SALAT

Dujie Tahat

SALAT

TUPELO PRESS
North Adams, Massachusetts

Library of Congress Catalog-in-Publication data available upon request.
ISBN-13: 978-1-946482-35-8

Cover image: Jordan Nassar, *A Lost Key*, 2019, Hand-Embroidered Cotton on Cotton,
    49.5 x 32.5 in.
Cover and text design by Ann Aspell.

First paperback edition November 2020

TUPELO PRESS
P.O. Box 1767
North Adams, Massachusetts 01247
(413) 664-9611 / Fax: (413) 664-9711
editor@tupelopress.org / www.tupelopress.org

Tupelo Press is an award-winning independent literary press that publishes fine fiction, non-fiction, and poetry in books that are a joy to hold as well as read. Tupelo Press is a registered 501(c)(3) non-profit organization, and we rely on public support to carry out our mission of publishing extraordinary work that may be outside the realm of the large commercial publishers. Financial donations are welcome and are tax deductible.

contents

SALAT

salat to define the terms of ritual

[adhan]

A calling, a culling, a billowing
minaret banner, a cigarette starter thrown
out a moving car window to prove a point.

[standing]

Rapt, trapped, evangelical
about the whole thing
really, hinged
on guilt and hoping
you'll sign the papers before
the door slams shut.

[bowing]

In lieu of communion, Father
crosses my forehead.
                    Irreverence
has somehow escaped the mouth,
and now we're discussing sincerity.

[prostration]

All this searching for my heart to be broken.

[prostration again]

You'll sleep when you die
but form is death. The gap
between   every prayer
is sleep. The joke is: no such
thing as sleep.

                    Dead be dead.

        [sitting]

On bare feet, on upturned
buckets, on an ice block
bombing down grassy
terraces, tears blessing
the angles of our return.

In our good clothes, shoulder
to shoulder in the pew,
in a broken down Chrysler
miles and miles from home.

        [salam alaikum]

Back to the work, if you're lucky,
hands unblemished still with grace.

salat on the first day of school

[adhan]

The bell rings and before I am introduced to my classmates, they recite in unison a pledge of allegiance to the flag.

[standing]

Before I become   the boy
with the funny name
I am the boy without   a name
standing at the front
of the classroom
waiting on the teacher
to speak. *My name is*
Carte Blanche!, I want
to shout, but my mouth
was busy   breathing.

[bowing]

At the drinking fountain, a boy's mouth
stained red asks if I want to play tag,
pointing in the direction of two
or three other red-stained boys.
Before I reply, he says, *you're it.*

I mistook their flash-
ing teeth for smiles.
Craving wildness, I ran
for the jungle
gym.

[prostration]

I must have fallen near the merry-
go-round before they came
with their feet and between the kickdrum
bangs, I made out, *Welcome to America, bitch!*

[prostration, again]

I pray silent
alone now.

[sitting]

I don't remember the words anymore—only the motions
my father made standing next to the x-ray machine. His hands
moved everywhere as the crosshairs on my chest closed in.

[salam alaikum]

So the day ends with three cracked ribs.
There are metaphors and then there are

metaphors. The angels on my shoulders
know I mean the latter.

salat as a portrait allowing my father to have grace and bad luck

[adhan]

I call upon peace-be-upon Ibrahim to bless him,
my father who is different from my pops the way a bar is
different from a rod depending on what
direction it's swung or what end the I is held.

[standing]

Of course, there is
so much empire
in my father's mind
could carve out extra; a buffer
zone for some other's
empire; look close enough and you can make
out the precision of a blade—a hatchet drawn,
a sliver of silver moon.

[bowing]

Ibrahim in the Palm Springs of Washington
swings a hammock smack dab in the dog
days of summer, crowned
in a valley of apples—honey and milk
runneth over like too much of a good thing
might make you want to kill
your brother, so he calls for his children.

[prostration]

During golden hour, at every sun's vanishing
point, his skin tint went
red, a sudden

arrangement of tomatoes
blossoming in his arms and chest—
each of us torn

from the root, half a fruit—
his maw dripping
mauve.

[prostration again]

When I say   *I say*
I mean, so when
I mean I say   *Ameen.*

When I say   *I mean*
I mean *Ameen.*

                                    Forgive me.

When I said
Ameen, I meant   mine.

[sitting]

In most waiting
       rooms, I place his
name next to mine.
       When asked what
it mean, I point
       to my own thinning
flesh and say
       with my whole
chest that there's a river
       in heaven, and I am
the star that belongs
       to it.

[salam alaikum]

I need you to believe me when I say my father
could cartwheel on a park bench keeping a cigarette

clenched in his teeth. Pops was equal parts dazzle and charm.
An Ibrahim with all '80s swagger. See them and know they'd done some shit.

[sitting]

Between bites, I unlock
my phone to search

as if I didn't already know
the meaning of the word negligence—

the way it ends by forcing air through
yet another set of teeth.

[salam ailaikum]

…ending with a closed mouth. Even
with all our modern contraptions, drowning remains
one of the most common ways to die.

Of course I praise the terror.

salat during deportation proceedings

[adhan]

The judge gets my name right this time—
the whole thing.

[standing]

Crossing the bar,
I follow my lawyer's
lead. I yes at everyone.
I'm sympathetic
to your argument,
the judge says. Yes.
But there's nothing
I can do. Yes.

[bowing]

Between jokes, my lawyer
asks me about my case
on the elevator
ride down.
He always
steps on
the punch line.

[prostration]

Desperation is the start of grief
is what I learned in a room like this,
watching it form in my father's fall
from his face to the floor; my mother
and sister unfazed at the sight of shame.

[prostration again]

It's always dramatic metaphor with family.

[sitting]

Pews and pews, lawyers and snakes—
even the unbelievers look for grace,

unpracticed, as I am, asking God
for any old thing to have blessed

the judge with a good moaning,
a lover just this morning at his knees.

[salam alaikum]

The order to appear in which body—
boy, husband, father. Leave them
all at home. That's the order of removal.

salat to be read from right to left

[adhan]

messages Facebook me sends uncle My
does translator Facebook .understand barely I
.ح with starts One .images to apply not

.amo ,you love I writes He

[standing]

,clothes Friday my In
skips he as me sees homie the
just is mosque The .school
from corner the round house a
.algebra period second

[bowing]

phone my over Hovering
7abibi why searching I'm
name pop's if as—habibi not and
.line the on weren't

[prostration]

.Rayan Al Dujanaht it's ,God of house wooden this In
even sometimes ,gate the at ,Dujie

different is father my ,Here .way the on
course Of .same the or
wild this ,prayer all it's

pushing ,corner the to jockeying
.another down back then ,out not up

[again prostration]

?this say to How

[sitting]

¹.God by Confounded

[alaikum salam]

direction which days these note I
foot what ,drip ablution of drops last the
,shoes my on back putting when first goes
.shut slams gate the how

الحمدلله ¹

salat in the name of the father

[adhan]

The sound of his name starts at the bottom of your throat
where it opens and the air settles the moment
before a word like adhan or allah or akbar floats
into the open dawn.

[standing]

My father is lodged in my throat,
bobbing as I swallow some
sign I wish to make
into myself to show
the kids at school
that I can be American. I can be
not like my pops—I mean papa.
He tightens round my neck
as a pair of baby blue high
tops slide on by. My hunger
for cable tv and any degree
of certainty insatiable.

[bowing]

I lean forward to lengthen
my neck, and my father sees me   as if
on an executioner's block.
I meant only to show off   the gold
chains some Arabs have come to be
known for in popular American
culture. O pops, I stretch
my throat like oil slick A-rab   money.

17

[prostration]

He appears smaller on his knees in the corner
of his kitchen, reaching round the knife
drawer. The pain is real, but the blade
against his throat is yet another
promise he will not keep.

[prostration again]

I want to tell you, friend, that where the pain is located
will reveal some wisdom, that our bodies know
best how to process the messiness of becoming. I want to
say that the throat is a place where it all comes to rest,
where I will find some finally in this utterance
but the threshold is still a floor.

[sitting]

Each of my children are coiled into the corners of my jaw
catching all the toxins, yet it seems the safest place to stow.
Where to keep them is a question
                                                    I ask as if I had a choice.

[salam alaikum]

I tell my daughter to point her finger up
when she says *happy*, to feel the air push
against the roof of her mouth. Then I show her to point
downward—as if into her hips—when saying   my middle name.
But before she aloud wonders
who that could be, what that name might
conjure, I ask if she can tell the difference.

salat in a dream with Jida's ghost on the night of Korryn Gaines' killing

[adhan]

My grandmother rings with laughter when I tell her about the time her son
      shotgunned
a cigarette down my toddler throat to wave me away from the smoke, from ready-
aim-fire, from busted down doors and standoffs.

[standing]

I'm shook. The room   shakes.
There is a faceless man
shaped like my father   at the door
and she refuses to let him in.
The stranger knocks louder.
Mushkili mushkili, she says.
We huddle together—   conspiring
over *The New York Times*
Sunday crossword
to find the word for   trouble.

[bowing]

She's bent over, bleary-eyed with laughter now
as the whole world becomes suspended
mist. I steady reach for something
solid—a door
knob only to find
rust. A fine dust

coating my
fingertips. *Jida,*
what is so funny?
Your son is dead
set on leaving
and nowhere
to be found.

      [prostration]

A familiar fear begins to pool between my knees;
it falls from my face to the floor, but this is no time
for prayer. Do everything just right, just the way
your parents did, and you still baptized by the bullet.

      [prostration, again]

The child that I am knows so little
about death. All my family keeps
dying before I ever get to meet them.

[sitting]

In my dream,
we eat on the floor.
She tells more jokes.
I laugh desperately.
We paint each other's hair
with mud. Jida's dry hands
always caked with flour.

[salam alaikum]

She gets up to leave, and I am four
again, hiding from her wet kiss
in the trunk of a car meant to take us
to our flight to America.

salat the morning after a terrorist attack

*— for the 50 Muslims killed in Christchurch, New Zealand
during Ju'mah on March 15, 2019*

[adhan]

My littlest's small hands ask if I'm okay
this holy Friday. The alarm rings, and, minutes after, still
looking up into the square light
of my phone:

I'm weeping.

[standing]

On the train ride to the airport,
my ex wife calls to say,   *Good news:*

no cancer.

and I'm weeping all over
myself again.

No one
seems to notice.

[bowing]

There's a baby   in a stroller

                              so I burst into tears.

Another's beloved's perfect   shoulder. A child   on an escalator.

        TSA
        asks if there are liquids
        in my bag and I burst

into tears   —sorry—I mean   I'm weeping, ma'am. Rifling

through my carry-on,   my contact   lens solution hits the floor,
and I'm sorry
                —I'm sorry—

I'm trying to put all this

                        water back   in my eyes.

        [prostration]

I count up to fifty
people on the plane,

and several are afraid
we're going to die.

I want to tell them:
We're all gonna die.

[prostration again]

I'm a stranger   in California.   I search
for the closest mosque   by listening
     for the weeping.

     The sermon:

We're all gonna die
     and it's a beautiful thing.
   May Allah
   make the angels   *at the time of your death*   *ones of mercy.*

Are we prepared to face allah subhanahu wa ta3alah?

[sitting]

I touch my people's knees.
I grace my people's elbows.
I hold my people's hands.
My people. My people. My people.

May allah subhannalah accept them.
     [salam alaikum]

I say to my perfect Santa Clara strangers:

Thank you, brother.

Thank you, sister,

And I never meant it more in my life. May allah subhanalah accept them.

salat during graveyard

[adhan]

A woman I've never met lifts her shirt up just minutes past
two a.m. hoping to convince me to look
past the illegal in a late night 40 of OE and I think for a moment
that this time I might.

[standing]

From just inside
the door enough that
the alarm chimes and chimes
and chimes and chimes, my guy shouts
for a spare cig, having
slogged his way to his third corner
store of the night. *They don't sell
looseys like they used to no more—
gotta buy the whole damn pack
at that* while my stiff
lip sticks one right
in the spittoon
bucket.

[bowing]

I pour myself over another wall of words I will not finish,
my face so close to a good book I don't notice
the man walk in who looks like my mother's
grandfather who worked the gas station

he owned in Tarlac till the very end
so this might be my birth and death
rite and as I consider the frightening
implication of how not that far everyone
I've ever loved has really made it, this man

who wants what's sold from under
the counter, unzips his sweater, reaches
into his abdomen and slaps his liver
onto the register as payment.

[prostration]

The homie whose name I never remember
but stays out back a bit to help flatten boxes
sometimes tries again tonight to pay

with pain pills, counting out each supplication
until he forgets what he came for. *Whatever*,
he says, *going to the VA on Friday*.

I want to tell him this one's on me,
but I say nothing—only slide the pills
back into the bottle when he's not looking.

[prostration again]

This is a poem about the people I grew to love
later, when I had had my fill. So if you have never

been this close to hunger—the kind that makes

you forget to feed your flesh—there is a vanishing
distance between all the ways we have ever prayed.

[sitting]

Between the hours
        of four and six a.m., I give
thanks to the minutes
        having softer edges
around which I twist
        and release my spine
after restocking cigarettes

        and refilling coffee pots.
In this stretch,
        it's mostly trabajadors
in hair nets and hard
        hats, armfuls of conchas
at the counter, and
        occasionally, a child

in a stroller pulling
        Takis out a little
crackling bag, and
        that staticky sound
of holiness compels
        me, but I stay squat
on my stack of crates.

[salam ailaikum]

After wiping down the gas pumps, when my hands no longer stick
with Pine-Sol and sawdust, I fire up the fryer and drop
the handfuls of pizza sticks and chicken strips

that will be served as breakfast. Soon I will drive home in the dark
and crawl into my daughter's bed as she stirs
at this redolence of grease.

salat as a youth of the world dancing and singing and imitating natural objects

[adhan]

I harmonize through this
busted tailpipe throat. My muffler
wheezes. I would say I swing like junk
yard dog but the mirrors of my mind are yet unbroken.

[standing]

Given the choice,
I make myself
a lake,
a babbling
brook slung
tongue
at the head.

[bowing]

I am at the base of some valley
flooding the sky with my face.
If you'll allow me to speculate
for a moment, I'd drown the blue
out myself. I am all red water, and no,
dear reader, there is no blood in this
poem. I will not let there be blood
in this poem.

[prostration]

What happens after all this is yours,
but this scrawling ripple stippled

tide is paleolithic past tense
bent round itself

till the ocean is all
that's left.

[prostration again]

Water and salt return
to water and salt.

[sitting]

If there were anyone left on this earth
to witness, they'd find the ruins of a used car
lot next to a liquor store at the edge of a small city
where my mother's bones still stay.

[salam alaikum]

Attend to this, o friend, this song,
this burial, this holy water be praised
stretching farther into the collapsing
distance than we ever could
have imagined.

notes

Salat, or salah, is the physical and spiritual act of prayer, which according to the five pillars of Islam is meant to be conducted five times a day.

"salat to define the terms of ritual" responds, in part, to Mary Reufle's essay "Kangaroo Beach"

"salat to be read from right to left" is written after Marwa Helal and her invented form, The Arabic, which she defines as the following: The Arabic is a form that includes an Arabic letter with an Arabic footnote, and an Arabic numeral, preferably written right to left as the Arabic language is, and vehemently rejects you if you try to read it left to right. To vehemently reject, in this case, means to transfer the feeling of every time the poet has heard an English as Only Language speaker patronizingly utter in some variation the following phrase: "Oh, [so-and-so] is English as a Second Language..." As if it was a kind of weakness, nah.

"salat the morning after a terrorist attack" references Fatimah Asghar's "If They Should Come for Us"

"salat as a youth of the world dancing and singing and imitating natural objects" paraphrases "Defence of Poetry" by Percy Bysshe Shelley and responds, in part, to Lena Khalaf Tuffaha's *Water and Salt* (Red Hen Press 2017)

acknowledgments

Big gratitude to the editors of the following publications, where many of these poems first appeared or are forthcoming: *Cordite Review*, *Cosmonauts Avenue*, *Grist*, *Hobart*, *Nashville Review*, *Nimrod*, *Ninth Letter*, *POETRY*, *Seventh Wave*, *Southern Indiana Review*, *Yemassee*.

"salat during graveyard," "salat departing LAX the week after an attempted terrorist attack," and "salat on the first day of school" appear in the forthcoming chapbook *Here I Am O My God*, selected by Fady Joudah as a winner of the Poetry Society of America Chapbook Fellowship.

These poems exist with eternal gratitude to so many more than I could ever name. I've always thought the greatest honor in writing poems is getting to be part of the choir, so here are a few living voices for whom I owe the thinking and crafting that led to this book: Daemond Arrindell, Bill Carty, Sarah María Medina, Gabrielle Bates, Luther Hughes, Troy Osaki, Lena Khalaf Tuffaha, Hanif Abdurraqib, Zeina Hashem Beck, Kaveh Akbar, Michael Dhyne, Ross Gay, José Olivarez, Fady Joudah, R.A. Villanueva, Marwa Helal, Solmaz Sharif, Fatimah Asghar, Rick Barot, Danez Smith, Yujane Chen, Jess Rizkallah, Vievee Francis, Matthew Olzmann, Eve L. Ewing, Nate Marshall, Amanda Torres and the whole Poetry Incubator fam, my cohorts at Jack Straw Writing Program and Hugo House, my workshop group at Bread Loaf Writing Conference as well as the last (and best) Bread Loaf Wait Class. I don't know what I did to deserve you all.

I continue to owe an immeasurable debt of gratitude to Emily Parzybok, my first reader and best friend. Thank you.

This work—as all the work is—is for Isabella, Max, and Maya. I love you.

Sunken Garden Poetry at Hill-Stead Museum

Sunken Garden Poetry began in 1992 in Farmington, Connecticut, with a single poetry reading in the magical setting of Hill-Stead Museum's Sunken Garden, drawing huge crowds even that first year. Since then the annual series has become one of the premiere and best-loved venues for poetry in the country, featuring the top tier of American poets as well as emerging and student writers from the region. From its inception more than twenty-five years ago, this poetry festival has given equal weight to the quality of text and the poet's ability to deliver an engaging, powerful, and entertaining experience in the unique theater of the Sunken Garden.

Out of the festival have grown competitions, year-round workshops and events, and an educational outreach to Hartford high schools. And while centered at Hill-Stead—with its beautiful views, Colonial Revival house, and priceless collection of Impressionist paintings—Sunken Garden Poetry now engages an ever-wider audience through a growing on-line presence; an online poetry journal, Theodate (now found at hillstead.org); public radio broadcasts; and an annual chapbook prize, co-published by Tupelo Press.

Sunken Garden Chapbook Poetry Prize

2020
Salat by Dujie Tahat
Selected by Cornelius Eady

2019
Diurne by Kristin George Bagdanov
Selected by Timothy Donnelly

2018
Flight by Chaun Ballard
Selected by Major Jackson

2017
Ordinary Misfortunes by Emily Jungmin Yoon
Selected by Maggie Smith

2016
Feed by Suzanne Parker
Selected by Jeffrey Levine and Cassandra Cleghorn

2015
Fountain and Furnace by Hadara Bar-Nadav
Selected by Peter Stitt

2014
We Practice For It by Ted Lardner
Selected by Mark Doty